My Journey to Motherhood:
Overcoming Infertility & Fibroid

How I gave birth at 40 after trying for 9 whole years

Ogechi Madukoma

Copyright:

My Journey to Motherhood: Overcoming Infertility And Fibroid: How I Gave Birth At 40 After Trying For Nine Whole Years © Madukoma Ogechi, 2020

Author's Details:

Madukoma Ogechi Glory

08025429153, 07067361360.

WhatsApp - 08029046605

Email - ogebaby777@yahoo.com

Facebook - Madukoma John Ogechi or ogechi.egwumba

Instagram - @ogechimadukoma, @glomajos

Twitter - @madukomajohnogechi

All rights reserved.

No part of this book may be reproduced, stored in a retrieval system, or transmitted in any form or by any means; electronic, mechanical, photocopying, recording or otherwise, without the prior written permission of the copyright owner.

Book Cover Design, Editing, and Publishing: **The Book Surgeons International**

09090885868, 07061082014

www.thebooksurgeons.com

Ilorin: Malhub, House 6, Agba dam Link Road, GRA, Ilorin.

Lagos: 11, Omololu Street, Amukoko, Lagos

Acknowledgment

I want to acknowledge everyone that made writing this book easy and that contributed to its success in one way or the other.

To my darling husband Madukoma John, who went through this journey with me, thank you for being a man of faith;

My parent and siblings who pray for me day and night and do all they can to ensure this day comes to be;

My in-laws who were patient with me through this journey, especially my father-in-law who went as far as "sowing seeds" for me, I don't take your love for granted;

My pastors and friends that were there to encourage me all through this journey, I thank God for blessing me with people like you;

To The Book Surgeons International for making writing a book so easy that I could start and finish as planned, you are doing great!

My Journey to Motherhood

To you who will buy and read this book, or gift it to someone that needs to read it, may God answer you quickly.

I appreciate you all for making this dream come true, God bless you abundantly.

Overcoming Infertility And Fibroid

Dedication

I dedicate this book to God Almighty, who gave me the story in this book and made it end in praise. He turned my story to glory, He gave us the grace to be patient and wait through the period. May His name be praised forever.

I also dedicate this to my husband, Madukoma John, who stood by me through the trying period and worked with me as a team. I will love you forever.

I dedicate this book to my daughter, Deborah Joy John Madukoma. You brought joy and laughter into our home and sunshine to our love life, God bless and keep you in Jesus mighty name.

Lastly, I dedicate this book to every couple out there battling with infertility. You are the reason I wrote this book and I pray that it will be the answer you have been waiting for as it propels you to take the appropriate action leading to your desired result.

It will surely end in praise by the grace of God almighty.

Foreword

My very first encounter with "Madam Ogechi" like I use to call her was in April 2020 when she joined our online Antenatal group "AskTheGynecologist".

She joins and goes "I am Madukoma Ogechi. I just joined this group and I hope to make the best use of what I will be learning here" and yeah, she sure did.

It was evident she is a reader from her many questions; the funny, the true, the myths, and all. I would laugh at some of her questions before answering but one thing stood out about her – she was a good student. She was willing to unlearn the wrong information and relearn the right ones.

She was indeed a mother/mama bear in the pregnancy. She didn't hesitate to carry out any investigation, get home monitor, etc.

Going through her story in this book shows a true reflection of what many women in our society go through and I'm happy she's willing to let others learn from her mistakes.

Many women in the waiting period try their hands on all sorts of herbs (which may damage their vital organs later in life) and do the things that work against their fertility because they are overwhelmed with the stress of waiting.

I pray more women will read this and differentiate the right from the wrong. I pray it revives hope in many women out there who are also going to conceive eventually.

Dr. Esther Oluwadeyi

M.B.ChB (OAU Ife)

Doctor; Ask the Gynecologist (ATG)

Introduction

Infertility is the monster affecting a lot of couples these days and it is becoming very common in our society.

What is infertility?

This is when a couple cannot achieve conception or stay pregnant over a twelve-month trying period despite regular unprotected sexual intercourse.

Recent global evidence shows infertility as a major public health problem. It is a problem of global proportion that affects between 8% and 12% of couples worldwide. In developing countries, about 25% of couples are infertile due to primary or secondary infertility. In Nigeria, the overall prevalence of infertility is 22% with primary infertility at 5% and secondary at 18%. This is according to a study conducted by the gynaecology unit of the Bowen University Teaching Hospital, Ogbomoso, Nigeria.

I battled this monster for 9 whole years and overcame it by the grace of God. That journey was very challenging but I learned many lessons. I especially thank God for the grace to be patient while He did His work.

I have written this book to share my story in its raw state and the lessons I learned in this journey so that you can learn from my mistakes and shorten the time of your waiting.

In the course of waiting and trying to conceive, I developed a fibroid which was a major health challenge but I overcame that.

This book will be a very good gift for any family or friend who is battling with infertility. We need to fight this monster together to reduce these statistics.

I am praying for everyone out there trying to conceive. As you take the appropriate action, you will get a favourable result by the grace of God sooner than you expect.

Baby dust to you as you celebrate and be celebrated in nine months.

Madukoma Ogechi

Overcoming Infertility And Fibroid

Table of Content

Acknowledgment

Dedication

Foreword

Introduction

1. Growing Up
2. My Marital Journey
3. My Fibroid Story
4. What Is Fibroid?
5. Myomectomy & Conception…
6. Infertility…
7. What Causes Infertility?

My Journey to Motherhood

8. The Journey To Our Laughter

9. Why Worry Over What You Don't Own?

10. God Answers Prayers

11. And It Happened…

12. And The Devil Came With Blighted Ovum…

13. And It's a Girl…

My Journey to Motherhood

Overcoming Infertility And Fibroid

1

Growing Up

—

I got married in 2010 to my friend who is now my lovely husband, at the age of 30. That is late, right? I will tell you why.

I was born into a middle-income family in Ajegunle. I had my primary and secondary education in Ajegunle. My parents did all they could to provide us with all that we needed. My mum was a petty trader at the popular Boundary market while my dad worked with Unilever, formerly Lever Brothers. We lived happily as a family even without a silver spoon as our parents provided most of our needs and never allowed our education to suffer. Even if they would joke with anything, it certainly wasn't our education. Although we attended government schools, they bought all our books and paid our levies. Things continued like this until my dad was retrenched at his place of work. He tried one or two businesses that didn't work out. Then we had to live on the proceeds from my mum's trade.

Our standard of living dropped but, being brought up to be contented with what we have, we managed. It was difficult though as many challenges came up. To feed adequately became a huge challenge but, thank God for my mum who had the type of Godly training that despite all these challenges, we kept our cool in Ajegunle, a kind of place that is known for all sorts of atrocities. The grace of God kept us from deviating.

Things continued like this until my elder brother graduated from secondary school and took up a job to support the family financially, knowing that furthering his education at that time was not feasible. My parents had to sell the fridge in our house at the time to pay for my WAEC examination fee even though it was highly subsidized for a government school.

After my WAEC examination, I was at home for some months, believing that my cousin abroad would send me money to further my education. Then I read a book by Bishop Oyedepo titled, Exploiting the Secret of Success. In that book, He makes it clear that what one needs to succeed in life has been deposited within the person and that nobody owes anyone anything, not even one's parents. If a parent chooses to send a child to school, it should be considered a privilege. I was

My Journey to Motherhood

about 18 years old at the time. These words stirred something in my young mind and I told myself not to wait anymore. I had to do something to help myself and my family. I decided I needed to get a job to save money to go back to school. Thank God I took that decision because, till today, that cousin I was looking up to have not asked me how I went about it.

I got a job in a fast-food restaurant in Ebute-Metta. I think my salary then was about N4, 000. I was working and believing in God to save money so that I could go back to school. However, I couldn't save enough because I had to support the family from that little salary, pay my transport fare to work and carry out other expenses. There were times that I had to pay the rent as young as I was. That made it difficult for me to accumulate savings.

I left the fast-food restaurant and got another job as a security lady with Bemil Securities. I was posted to work at Africa-re insurance. At Africa-re, I was posted to work at the reception and I had a lot of time to read. I made great friends there and so many people encouraged me. While there, I noticed some staff working and schooling at the same time. I realized I could do the same, instead of waiting to save enough. God brought people my way and that made my decision easier. Also, I had decided that I wasn't going to get married until I got a tertiary education. I was around 25 years old when I

Overcoming Infertility And Fibroid

My Journey to Motherhood

eventually got admitted at Ambrose Alli University, Edo state. They had a sandwich program here in Lagos. We attended lectures over the weekend and went over to the main campus when it was examination time. We stayed there for one month, did revisions, and wrote our exams. Even though I was not entitled to annual leave at the time, God favored me and I was granted permission for a whole month to go write my exams when it was time. My bosses saw me as a young lady from the notorious Ajegunle area, struggling to succeed so they supported me.

By the grace of God, I graduated with a B.Sc. in Economics in 2009. I was 29 at the time. After my education, I got married in 2010, at 30. At this time, I had achieved my dream of getting a university education. I had moved from Africa-re insurance to a three-star hotel in Lekki. Even though I was employed as a security lady at the gate, I didn't work for up to three months there before I was moved to the store to work as the store assistant. By that time I was leaving one month before my wedding in August 2010, as the Stores/Purchasing Manager. I rose from being a security lady to being a store assistant and then to the manager of a department. I also had my certificate as a graduate in Economics and today by the grace of God, I own my business, Glomajos Enterprises, where we produce various household cleaning products.

Overcoming Infertility And Fibroid

My Journey to Motherhood

Each time I look back at my journey, I give God all the glory. These challenges kept me going because of my decision not to get married without at least a university education. I thought the challenges were over until I was faced with infertility after getting married for nine years.

I am about to take you on a journey on how we faced these challenges and overcame them. If we did overcome, you too will. Come along with me as I take you on this journey. I pray that as you read, you will find solutions to your challenges also in Jesus' name. No matter what the challenge is; marital, financial, educational, etc. Remember that "winners don't quit and quitters don't win". Just keep pushing and sooner than you expect, you will testify.

You can imagine how happy I was when I delivered my product, Loryma toilet bowl cleaner, to Africa-re insurance in December 2018. They were going to use it as a Christmas gift to their staff, and some of these staff members were there when I worked as a security lady. By the grace of God, they would be using a product that has my name on it in their homes.

No matter what you are going through now, no matter your background, you can still make it to the top. Just keep at what you are doing and in due time, you will reap the reward.

Overcoming Infertility And Fibroid

2

My Marital Journey

—

I got married in September 2010 and settled in with my love to build our new home. I had lost my job with the hotel for exactly one month to my wedding which was held in August 2010. I had to stay at home for a while and my husband resumed work at the expiration of his leave.

The clock began to tick. We started trying to have a baby. Like it is the practice in this part of the world, people began to count the months for. Slowly, months turned into years. We marked our first wedding anniversary. We were not worried yet at this time as we reassured ourselves that it is just the first year, after all, it would happen the second year, we hoped.

By this time, I had got a job as a secondary school teacher in a private school nearby to keep myself engaged while I

My Journey to Motherhood

continued my job search. Being a person that hates sitting at home, and for the loneliness that I feel in the absence of my husband, I thought I should stay in the school for a term, at least.

When we were almost six months into the second year of our marriage, our relations started asking questions, especially our parents who were getting worried already. We also began to worry because we didn't know what was wrong but we had always trusted God and His word which promises us that he that finds a wife, finds a good thing, and obtains favor from God. We would pray, quoting His word and telling Him to favor our marriage with children, reminding Him that He said none shall be barren, reminding Him of His word in Gen. 1: 28 that we should be fruitful and multiply and replenish the earth. Before we knew it, our second wedding anniversary came.

Our worries grew as people continued asking questions like "When are we coming to eat rice?" "What are you guys waiting for? We want to come for naming." Some that could not ask us directly started talking, even in the church.

I remember an incident where someone had just given birth in the church. This couple had also waited for about two years before they gave birth to their son and coincidentally, we got

Overcoming Infertility And Fibroid

married the same year. We got married in September while they got married in December of 2010.

After the naming ceremony, a youth from the church visited me. As we were chatting, she said, "People are saying that thank God that so and so sister has given birth; now it remains sister Oge." When she said that, I felt like crying but I held the tears. Each time I heard such, I went back to God and cried to Him, reminding him of his words. The boy that was given birth to, that year, clocked seven years by June 2020. The lady that paid me that visit got married later and had 3 children while we were waiting.

We waited, prayed, and trusted God. We had not gone to the hospital to find out if there was any problem because we believed we were okay and that it was just a matter of a little time before God would bless us with the fruit of the womb. We were expecting God to play His part but we failed to play ours by going to the hospital having waited for over two years. We neglected the fact that the doctors were there to help us. God gave them wisdom and solutions to our health problems. We should seek their help when the need arises.

One day, when we were well into the half of the third year, my husband told me that we would be going to see a herbal doctor which his colleague had told him about. The herbal doctor had given my husband's friend some herbs when he had the same challenge we did. He told my husband that after he consumed the herbs, his wife became pregnant.

With faith, we went to the herbal doctor's place in Ikorodu. We informed him that we had been married for over two years with no child. He billed us and we paid. He then gave us some herbs and instructed us on how to use them. We thanked him and left. We used the herbs as instructed. We used all of the herbs and went back for more. After taking the herbs for a while without a favourable result, we got tired and decided not to go there for more.

Back at home, the wait continued. Before we knew it, our third wedding anniversary came and we were still waiting and believing God for our children.

It was after our third wedding anniversary that I noticed that my monthly menstrual flow became very heavy. Each month, I bled like the woman with the issue of blood in the Bible. I didn't know that some other health challenges had set in. I was forced to go to the hospital when the bleeding became unbearable. I wanted to find out what the cause of this bleeding was. Come with me to chapter three.

Overcoming Infertility And Fibroid

3

My Fibroid Story…

—

I was bleeding heavily each month that I was getting worried not knowing why my menstrual flow suddenly got this heavy.

At work one day, in our warehouse at Apapa, we were offloading one of our 40ft containers. At a restaurant where we usually ate near the warehouse, I sat there watching the off loaders as they offloaded our products from the container into the warehouse.

I was wearing blue jean trousers, though I didn't wear trousers regularly, I liked wearing one each time I was going to the warehouse because of the nature of the work there. I sat down in one of the plastic seats in the restaurant watching as they offloaded. At a point, I had to stand up to observe what was going on inside the warehouse. Immediately I came out, I saw the sales boy at the restaurant and two other customers discussing, looking at the seat I just stood up from

My Journey to Motherhood

and pointing at me. I went closer to find out why they were pointing at me only to notice heavy bloodstains on the seat I just got up from. I turned to look at my trousers and it was also stained with blood. I had to apologize and offer to wash the seat but the boy said I shouldn't worry. He poured water over it and washed it.

I knew I was menstruating and I used a pad. However, I didn't know my pad had become so full that it leaked through my jean trousers unto the chairs. It was in the morning and the container arrived the previous day so I resumed straight at the warehouse to offload before noon to avoid paying demurrage.

Thank God I had a Cardigan with me. I had to cover my stained jean with it. I then went straight home after we finished offloading instead of going back to the office. I became very worried. I called an aunt of mine who is a midwife and she asked me to come for her to examine me. I told my husband when he came back from work that day and he suggested I should rather go to the clinic. I went to the clinic the next day and complained. I was examined and asked to go for a scan which I did. The scan revealed that I had a fibroid. I never expected the diagnosis and I felt so unhappy about it.

Overcoming Infertility And Fibroid

My Journey to Motherhood

I went to the doctor with the result. He looked at it and told me that the cause of the bleeding was fibroid but also assured me that it was not too much for me to worry about. At that time, it was just about 0.9cm wide. I asked if that could be the cause of my inability to conceive for three years but he said no. The fibroid at that stage was too small to cause infertility. I was relieved to hear that the fibroid was not the cause of my inability to conceive and I went home thereafter.

As the months went by, the bleeding increased. I started using double heavy flow pads. Yet, I got stained anytime I went out during my menstrual period. I stopped wearing any other color of gown during my menstruation except black. I would wear only black for the whole of the 5 days. From 5 days, it extended to 7 days and started affecting my activities. I dreaded it each time my monthly cycle was approaching.

I suffered so much until one day in 2015. By this time, I had stopped working and started my own business. I had my factory in Ikorodu, close to my office. I saw a signpost where they wrote "REMOVE FIBROID WITHOUT SURGERY."

I decided to go in and make inquiries because before now, most of the reading and research I made online about fibroid referred to surgery as the most potent cure but we were afraid of surgery because of all the rumours about it and the fear that any woman that undergoes surgery would not be able to conceive afterward. So you can imagine how relieved I was to learn that I could remove this fibroid without surgery.

On further inquiry, I learned it's a drug from a Chinese company. Let me not mention the name here, but it is from one of the network marketing companies that claim that one drug can do so many things. I met with their representative in Ikorodu who took me to their head office at Ikeja to attend one of their lectures. During the lecture, I met with medical doctors that corroborated the story of the potency of these drugs. I left that lecture that day a believer as they succeeded in winning me over. I believed that I could get rid of the fibroid with these drugs, little did I know that I was going from the frying pan to fire.

Immediately we came back from their head office, I went to a woman who was to be my up-line to register and pay for these drugs. These drugs were very expensive. I bought so much for a complete dose that will shrink the fibroid and that will make me pass it out during my next menstrual period, according to her. I also bought some fertility drugs both for myself and for my hubby with the claim that the drugs would aid fertility. I never knew I was buying more trouble with my money.

I started taking the drugs at a six-hour interval as prescribed. I took it religiously, yet I didn't see any positive results.

My Journey to Motherhood

However, I kept taking it with an assurance from the woman that it would shrink. This was in 2015, five years into the marriage without conceiving and battling with fibroid. Instead of improvements, the situation became worse. At a point, I dared not go out on the second day of my menstrual period. I had to stay at home to change my pad almost every hour. I could use up 5 packs of Always Ultra in each cycle; wasting more money, time, and blood.

I was in class one day at the Enterprise Development Centre when I got a scholarship from the World Bank to study there. I didn't know one of my course mates had noticed that I drank a liquid in a small bottle from occasionally. She approached me during a break one day and asked what it was that I was always taking. I had to open up and told her that I had fibroid and I was taking those to treat the fibroid. I can never forget her response to me that day; she was very blunt and straightforward. She said, "Oge, if you have fibroid, go and remove it through surgery, all these things you are taking won't help."

I thanked her and left. But did I go for the surgery? NO! The fear of surgery was still in me. Instead, I continued with my medication from my up line, spending a whole lot of money. Instead of the menstrual flow to reduce, it became worse. I would bleed for twelve straight days with the thick blood clot. I suffered just like the woman with the issue of blood in the

Bible. This affected my daily activities a lot as I had to cancel so many appointments especially those that fell on the second day of my menstrual period. You won't believe that I had to stand throughout the service each time I went to church on Sunday during my period because I knew for sure that I would stain both the chair and my cloth if I dared to sit down. So to avoid causing a scene, I had to stand. I would join the ushering department during the church service and I would squat whenever I got tired of standing.

Do you know that on other days, I went about with an extra big scarf? Why? Each time I was going on public transportation, I would stylishly put this scarf on the seat before sitting down and also quickly remove it and put it in my already opened handbag immediately I got up in order not to stain the seat. Remember I was already wearing a black skirt. So it wouldn't be obvious if the skirt got stained. I couldn't even sleep on the bed any more during my menstrual period because no matter what, the bedspread will be stained by the time I woke up. I would rather sleep on the floor so that even if the floor got stained, I would mop it when I woke up. It was easier than washing the stained bedspread each morning.

I suffered during this period as a result of ignorance and fear. No wonder the Bible says, "My people perish for lack of knowledge." I suffered like this for 4 years, up to 2017 when

My Journey to Motherhood

God sent someone that came to encourage me to go and have it removed through surgery, assuring me that his wife also had a surgery to remove fibroid after they tried to conceive for about six years, and after which they had two boys. This gave me courage and hope. I told my husband and we agreed that I had to get it removed which I eventually did in August 2017, and you know what? The money I spent on the surgery was just about half of what I had spent on the other drug from my up-line. I wasted my money, my time, and suffered a lot because of my ignorance. This is what informs my writing this book so that someone out there will not go through what I went through. Those four years was hell. After the surgery, it was as if my life was handed back to me.

I will share the whole fibroid surgery story of myomectomy in the next chapter, just come along with me. I hope you are learning a thing or two from my experience, as that is the essence of writing this book. Just keep reading and learn from me so that you don't waste time, money, and also suffer ignorantly.

4

What Is Fibroid?

Uterine fibroid is a noncancerous growth of the uterus that often appear during childbearing years. It is also called leiomyoma (la-yo-ma-yo-mah) or myoma. Uterine fibroids aren't associated with an increased risk of uterine cancer and seldom develop into cancer.

My Journey to Motherhood

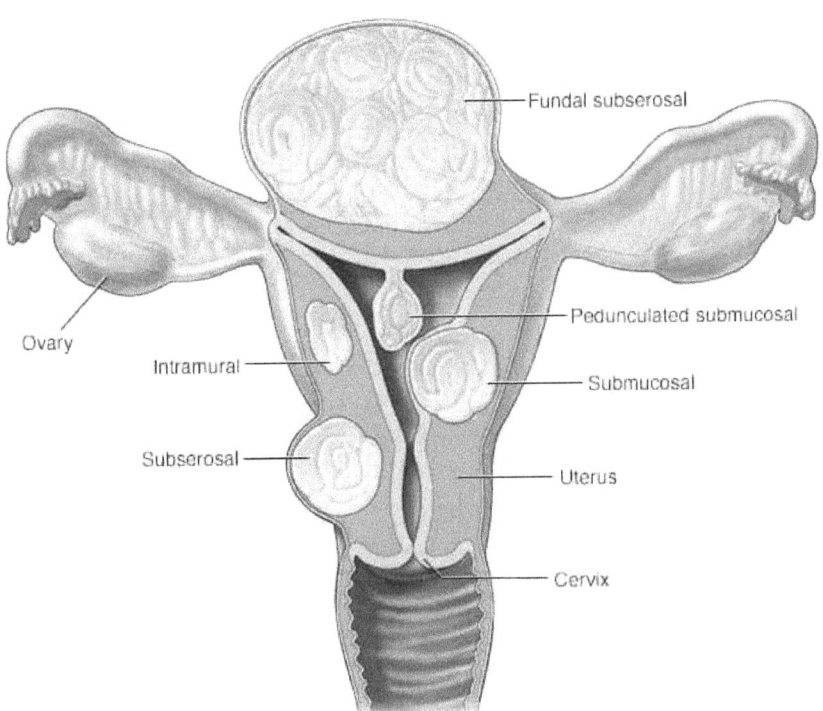

Fibroids come in a range of sizes from seedlings that are undetectable by the human eye to bulky masses that can distort and enlarge the uterus. You can have a single fibroid or multiple ones. In extreme cases, multiple fibroids can expand the uterus so much that it reaches the rib cage and can add weight to the body.

Overcoming Infertility And Fibroid

Symptoms

Many women who have fibroids don't show the symptoms. Its symptoms can be influenced by location, size, and several fibroids.

In women who have symptoms, the most common signs and symptoms of uterine fibroids include:

- Heavy menstrual bleeding;
- Menstrual periods that last for more than a week;
- Pelvic pressure or pain;
- Frequent urination;
- Difficulty emptying the bladder;
- Constipation;
- Backache or leg pains.

Types of Uterine Fibroids and where they can be found

- Intramural fibroids grow within the muscular uterine wall;

- Submucosal fibroids bulge into the uterine cavity;

- Subserosal fibroids project to the outside of the uterus. Some subserosal or submucosal fibroids may be pedunculated — hanging from a stalk inside or outside the uterus.

When to See a Doctor

See your doctor if you have:

- Pelvic pain that doesn't go away;

- Overly heavy, prolonged or painful periods;

- Spotting or bleeding between periods;

- Difficulty emptying your bladder;

- Unexplained low red blood cell count (anemia).

My Journey to Motherhood

Source: The Mayo Clinic

Back to my story, what I had was a submucosal fibroid. It was right in the uterine cavity that is located inside the womb. That was why I was bleeding like no man's business. At apoint, I became anemic. I would become very dizzy to an extent that I felt like fainting. If I climbed any stairs, you would see me panting and my heart beating fast like a deer chasing after water.

After my friend came, he told me about his wife that also had surgery after which they had two boys. My husband and I agreed that I should go for the surgery at either a government hospital or a teaching hospital. So we settled for Lagos University Teaching Hospital (LUTH).

I was given a referrer letter to LUTH from our clinic in January 2017. They received my history of both the cases of bleeding and infertility. When I met with the consultant who decided to carry out a scan himself to see the position of the fibroid. The result showed that the fibroid was right inside the womb and was now multiple. The fibroid had grown bigger to about 5.7cm as against its size of less than 1 cm before I started taking those drugs.

I didn't tell you that after the drug episode, I was referred to another woman that said she could shrink the fibroid using

Overcoming Infertility And Fibroid

native herbs. I agreed and paid. She asked me to come back the next day with a bottle of Schnapps. I did, and she prepared the medicine which I went home with. When I got home, I took this herbal mixture in alcohol. Immediately, I went blank, fell on the floor, and slept off. It took over an hour before I could get back to my feet. After then, I consumed it a couple of times and reacted the same way. I had to stop and throw it away. This was before we decided to go for the surgery.

Back at LUTH, the consultant decided he would need to remove the fibroid first before commencing the infertility treatment. When the record was checked to see when I could be booked for the surgery, the next available date was in June. Remember, this was in January. We waited in a queue because we had agreed to undergo the surgery done at LUTH. The surgery was eventually carried out on the 28th of August 2017. Some things happened in between which caused the surgery to be postponed twice even after I had been admitted on both occasions. I had to go back home on both occasions. You can imagine the emotional stress I went through on those occasions. I prepared myself and my mind for a surgery slated for the next Monday. I was admitted on Friday evening and Monday, a doctor came to me and told me that the surgery could not be done again.

Overcoming Infertility And Fibroid

My Journey to Motherhood

On one of those occasions, I had already been transfused with two pints of blood in readiness for the surgery only for my assigned anesthetist to take my pulse, write something on my file, and leave. On Sunday evening, my doctor came the next morning to tell me that the anesthetist said I could not be taken to the theatre because my pulse was lower than normal. I had to be discharged that morning and sent to go and do about 3 different tests and. In the end, the test result showed that nothing was wrong with me. Why my pulse was low to about 40 beats per minute, I can't say. I was rescheduled for another two weeks. I menstruated in between and I lost one whole pint of blood from just one menstrual period. I had to be transfused with another 3 pints of blood after the surgery before I became stable. In total, I took 5 pints of blood but I thank God that the surgery was a success without a complication to date.

I became free from fibroid after the surgery to date and I thank God for sending my friend to me the same way He is sending me to you who is going through the same challenge and reading this book. Don't wait to suffer for many years as I did because of fear and ignorance. You now know what to do. take that action today and become free from fibroid. God will help you through His grace.

Overcoming Infertility And Fibroid

5

Myomectomy & Conception

—

Each time I mention that I have had a myomectomy especially on some Facebook group pages, the next question is always; "Have you been able to conceive after the surgery?" Thank God that I can respond in the affirmative.

Myomectomy is a type of surgery used to remove uterine fibroids. There is this myth that a woman cannot conceive after a fibroid surgery which is what has kept so many women in the bondage of fibroid. Many are suffering in silence because they were told that they would not conceive if they go for surgery. Hence, they try to manage the fibroid using herbs to supposedly shrink it. Most times, that does not happen and they continue to suffer. Thus, increasing the magnitude of the problem.

My Journey to Motherhood

I remember when I was going to have this surgery. On my way to the hospital, I got a call from one of my cousins. She asked me to hold on for somebody and that person happens to be one of her pastors, a female. She started the conversation saying that my cousin told her that I am on my way to get surgery done because of fibroid. She said I should not go ahead with the surgery but go back home and get closer to God. She claimed God Himself would heal me because if I go ahead with the surgery, I may not be able to conceive after then.

This is was when I started this process of having this myomectomy done in January only to wait till August before it finally got to my turn and someone is telling me to go back home not minding the suffering I had been through as a result of the fibroid. Thank God for knowledge. I replied that she should not bother about me, that I would be fine, and that I will also conceive right after the surgery. I told her that she may be a pastor but she is not God to decide who conceives or not. The conversation ended and I felt sad after that. I was on my way to the hospital to have the surgery that would put an end to an illness that made me suffer and lost so much blood for many years and here was a pastor that was telling me to go back home instead of calling to pray for me. I went ahead and I had the surgery done. It was successful without complications and I was discharged about 4 days later. My

Overcoming Infertility And Fibroid

My Journey to Motherhood

healing was very smooth and fast that in less than one month, I returned to work doing the little things I could do with caution while I healed. Thank God that today, as against what she said, I got pregnant two years after the surgery.

I was coming back from my antenatal class one day at 35 weeks of pregnancy and decided to stop at the market to get the few things left from my hospital list. Luckily, l got what I wanted from one shop. During our interaction, the shop keeper got to know that this is my first pregnancy. I asked for a particular item, she was trying to describe it to me and I told her that I knew exactly what the product was and that I had used it before. She became curious and wanted to find out what I used it for. I told her that I used it when I had a fibroid surgery two years earlier. She started dancing and praising God. I was so surprised by her reaction that I asked her why she was dancing. She said the fact that I had a fibroid surgery and I was able to get pregnant was a miracle. She said that she used to believe that any woman who had a fibroid surgery wouldn't get pregnant. I told her that it is not true and began to educate her, citing other cases I knew of – people that had the surgery, and later had their children. I told her that even if she would not believe those cases at least she could see that I am a living testimony. The fibroid surgery does not stop one from getting pregnant, instead, enhances it, especially if the

Overcoming Infertility And Fibroid

fibroid is Sub mucosa like mine that was right inside the womb.

She appealed to me to spread this message and let other women know and also educate as many women as I could because according to her, the general belief out there is that it is very difficult for a woman to conceive after a fibroid surgery. I told her that I was already writing a book so that others could read and learn from my experience. Thank God that you are reading this book now. I pray you to learn from my experience and shorten your waiting time. You must not wait for 9 years as I did. If I had all the information I have now, I am sure that I would not wait that long. You can conceive after a fibroid surgery if you do the right thing. So put away that fear and do what you should do today. I see you carrying your baby by the grace of God Almighty.

What causes Fibroids?

Doctors don't know the cause of uterine fibroids but research and clinical experience point to these factors:

Genetic changes

Many fibroids contain changes in genes that differ from those in normal uterine muscle cells.

Hormones

Estrogen and progesterone, two hormones that stimulate the development of the uterine lining during each menstrual cycle in preparation for pregnancy appear to promote the growth of fibroids.

Fibroids contain more estrogen and progesterone receptors than normal uterine muscle cells do. Fibroids tend to shrink after menopause due to a decrease in hormone production.

Other growth factors

Substances that help the body maintain tissues such as the insulin-like growth factor, may affect fibroid growth.

Source: The Mayo Clinic

6

Infertility

—

Infertility is defined as the inability to get pregnant despite having frequent, unprotected sex for at least a year for most couples. It may result from an issue with either you or your partner or a combination of factors that prevent pregnancy.

Fortunately, many safe and effective therapies significantly improve your chances of getting pregnant. Infertility is a great challenge but thanks to God for science, there are many treatments for infertility these days. All we have to do is stand up and take action. Remember that you can continue doing the same thing the same way and expect to get different results.

Overcoming Infertility And Fibroid

My Journey to Motherhood

There are many options that you can choose from. Even if you have tried one option and failed, you have to keep trying until you achieve your desired result.

Around our 5th year of marriage, after we had tried so many treatments especially herbs without a result, we got tired and stopped. I had to stand up again and start to seek a solution. I went to the hospital and was asked to carry out various tests, some of which cost a lot of money. I had to do them. At a point, I realized that I was the only one going for this test; Oga has stopped going. He had not had a test done in a long time. Each time I did this test and took them back to the doctor, he just prescribed drugs without explaining what the issues were. For a long time, I just kept going without really knowing what my diagnosis was.

I had this discussion with my husband one day and pleaded with him to see the need to go run a test also. It took time but he eventually did. He went to LUTH to see a doctor with the result and was told that he would need surgery to correct a certain vain that is passing through the wrong place, and causing the abnormal temperature in that region. The doctor said that until it's corrected, the sperm in the semen would keep dying. They called it varicocele.

Varicocele is a swelling in the veins that drain the testicle. It's the most common reversible cause of male infertility.

Overcoming Infertility And Fibroid

My Journey to Motherhood

Although the exact reason that varicoceles cause infertility is unknown, it may be related to abnormal testicular temperature regulation. Varicoceles result in reduced sperm quality.

This was before I had my surgery. We were afraid. We did some consultations with other doctor friends and our pastors. In the end, we agreed he should go for the surgery if this would be the solution to his infertility.

He went back to the doctor and was booked for the surgery. We made all payments, and the surgery was done without complications. We were happy. We thought the mountain had been removed and that I could now conceive but that was not the case. We tried for another two years without success before the issue of the fibroid came up. I had my surgery for fibroid about two years later and we were hoping that we would get that positive test result but it wasn't happeningsoon. Sincerely, we got frustrated. When my husband was asked to carry out another test after my surgery, he was not willing. Will you blame him? After all, we've been through, I didn't give up. I was optimistic that it would surely happen someday.

When I had the surgery, the doctor said everything was fine with me though one tube was blocked and that was not a problem since I could conceive with just one. We waited for

Overcoming Infertility And Fibroid

yet another year and nothing happened. This was around the eighth year. Indeed, we went through a lot but I thank God for giving us the patience to wait on Him.

I wish to use this opportunity to encourage male folks, our husbands, to please always be ready to go for testing as soon as possible as this might help in reducing our waiting time. It takes two to tango. Infertility can affect either a male or a female but most times you see the women going from hospital to hospital, spending money and doing one test or the other while the man is relaxing believing that nothing is wrong with him without confirming with a test. If trying to conceive, a couple should come together and fight infertility couples rather than allowing the woman alone to be the one bearing the burden. That way, the waiting time will not belong.

Couples are generally advised to seek medical help if they are unable to achieve pregnancy after a year of unprotected intercourse and this should be done together.

Overcoming Infertility And Fibroid

7

What Causes Infertility?

―

Infertility can be caused by many factors including complications with egg or sperm production, genetic factors, age, or too much exposure to certain chemicals and toxins.

In rough terms, about one-third of infertility cases can be attributed to male factors and about one-third of factors affect women. For the remaining one-third of infertile couples, it is caused by a combination of problems in both partners and in about 20 percent of cases, is unexplained.

For a woman to become pregnant, at least four things have to happen:

1) A woman must produce and release a healthy egg from one of her ovaries (ovulation).

My Journey to Motherhood

2) A man must produce a healthy sperm that can successfully fertilize the woman's egg (fertilization).

3) The egg must travel through a fallopian tube towards the uterus (transportation).

4) The fertilized egg must be attached to the inside of the uterus (implantation).

This process does not follow through in many couples trying to conceive, hence the delay. However, the good news is, infertility can be treated.

How is infertility treated?

Infertility treatment will depend on the following:

1) What's causing infertility;

2) How long you've been infertile;

3) Your age and your partner's age;

4) Personal preferences.

Overcoming Infertility And Fibroid

My Journey to Motherhood

In most infertility cases, 85 to 90 percent are treated with conventional therapies, such as drug treatment or surgical repair of reproductive organs.

There are 3 main types of fertility treatment:

1) Medicines

2) Surgical procedures

3) Assisted conception – including intrauterine insemination (IUI) and In Vitro Fertilization (IVF)

You might need to see your doctor to decide the best option for you.

Back to our story, we tried many things that never worked for us but we kept on trying. We used herbs that we got from different herbal doctors by recommendation. There was a time we were sent a honey mixture medication from Warri Delta State, Nigeria to Lagos. We paid heavily and also paid for it to be sent down. Yet, nothing happened.

We visited a medical doctor that asked us to bring about 2 liters of lime juice with which he prepared an herbal concoction for us and for which we paid heavily. He was a practicing Orthodox doctor that had a hospital opened to the public. He was the first medical doctor I had ever seen that believed in the use of herbs. We drank the concoction, following his prescription but in the end, nothing happened. This was even before I had the fibroid surgery. This doctor boasted that the herbal concoction would take care of the fibroid and that I would not need surgery after taking the concoction. However, the fibroid got worse.

Also, I went to Ibadan to hold empowerment training for about a thousand women. I thought them how to produce various household cleaning products that they could sell and make money to put food on their table. While there, my friend and co-trainer complained of rheumatism and bought herbs from a herb seller opposite the hotel where we were lodged. After taking it, she attested to the efficacy of the herbs as she felt better. I approached the seller who was a Muslim cleric and related the challenge we were going through with infertility and asked if he could also prepare herbs for us. He responded in the affirmative and gave me a testimony of so many of his clients that had the same challenge who got the result after using his herb. I told him I would get back to him since I needed to discuss with my husband and get his approval before purchasing it.

I got back to Lagos, discussed with hubby and he gave his approval. I called the herbal doctor, paid and he sent the herbs to us by waybill. We took it religiously but in the end,

My Journey to Motherhood

there was no result. At this time we were trying everything we could to get the result we desired. You can't keep doing the same thing and expect a different result. Even in life, you have to do all you can to get your desired result. You just keep pushing and don't quit because "winners never quit and quitters never win". Remember that this was around the 8th year, yet, we refused to give up.

I had brought up the option of IVF but my hubby was not buying to it. To me, IVF was another option that we could explore. At a point, I even suggested adoption but he refused because he believed that change would come soon. I thought we could adopt while we waited for our change but since I couldn't do that alone, I had to give it up. The good thing is, we were working together through this. We knew we were in this boat together and for us to achieve the result we desired, we must fight it together. This is what a couple should do. Infertility is a big monster that I don't wish for anyone and it should be fought in every positive way, (no desperation please) till we achieve the result while also praying to God for his mercies and intervention.

I pray that God in His infinite mercy will look on every couple going through this challenge called infertility and give us victory over it and bring laughter into our homes. God will surprise us all soonest by His grace as I see baby and laughter in every home battling this monster.

Overcoming Infertility And Fibroid

8

The Journey To Our Laughter

—

Thanks so much for reading up to this point. Let me now share how we eventually overcame this monster called infertility after 9 whole years of waiting.

Before now, we prayed a lot about this challenge because we believed that it is only God that could turn the tide for us. Once, I had gone with a group to pray in a mountain in Osun state. My husband also went for deliverance services at Prayer City of The Mountain of Fire and Miracles Campground with days of fasting and prayer concerning the even though we were Redeemed members. We went to the redeemed camp several times just to pray because we believed that it is God that gives children and not any herbalist or any other god. So, anywhere they call on this true God, we were ready to go and pray.

My Journey to Motherhood

We were still in search of results till 2018 when one of my friends told me that she attended a particular church program in the Ebute area of Ikorodu, Lagos Nigeria. I started attending with her since it was just to pray. In January 2019, this church had its annual beginning of the year program that they call "Over to God". It was a 21-day fasting and prayer program to hand over the new year to God.

The theme of the program for the year 2019 was "The wonders of Mercy", so all the teachings and prayers for that year were centered on mercy.

It was in the course of that program that I got a call from my friend again, the one that encouraged me to go have surgery to remove my fibroid then, yes, Mr. Charles, my angel in human form in the course of this battle. He called me one day in January 2019 to wish me a happy new year. After the exchange of pleasantries, he asked: "Oge, how far with this infertility issue?" I told him that it seemed my hubby was getting fed up especially since after my surgery and many other treatments we had after it and had not yielded any positive result. He asked that I give him my husband's number which I did and he called him. Before now, he had told me of a doctor in the Mushin area of Lagos Nigeria where they had gone for treatment after his wife's fibroid surgery. It was "Baba" as we call him that treated them until she conceived and by the grace of God, they had two boys after waiting for about 6 years. So he called my husband and they talked. He then called me later to say that he had spoken with my husband and he had agreed to go see Dr. Ajayi (Baba).

When my husband came back that day, I asked if Mr. Charles called him, he said, "yes" and that I could go to Baba the next day to book an appointment with him. I was so happy from that moment onwards.

I went to see Dr. Ajayi the next day. He asked us both to come the following day with our previous test results. Early the next day, he went through the results and told us what the issues could be. Mine was just hormonal imbalance. He billed us and told us that he would commence treatment when we made the payment, even in installments. We made a part-payment the next day and he started the treatment.

For the first month, we were going to Baba's office for about 3 times a week for injections. His office was between Mushin and Ilasa in Lagos while we resided around the Mile 12 Owode-onirin. However, each morning, we would go there first for injections before going to work. We were spending time, resources, and energy but we kept going. After the first month, he did a confirmatory test and told us that there was an improvement. He reduced our injections to twice a week for another one month after which he carried out another test and he was impressed with the result. From the third month,

Overcoming Infertility And Fibroid

we were going just once a week and we did that for another 6 months. Was that easy? No, not at all. But we persisted. Thank God for my friend Mr. Charles that already told us that they went there for about 8 months before they got a result.

Each time it seemed like we were getting discouraged, I would remind my hubby that Mr. Charles went there for eight good months before they got a result so, we shouldn't be discouraged. Thank God for Baba who was a very godly man. Apart from treating us, he would counsel us, pray with us, and encourage us. He would tell you to always make yourself happy and that there should be joy in your home. He was a father indeed – much more than a doctor. Each time you got there with the slightest bit of worry, he would notice and ensure you were happy by the time you were leaving.

I remember going there one day downcast and unhappy. I was becoming worried because the treatment was taking too long. The anticipation and joy with which we started the treatment was waning. Immediately I got to him, he noticed and was asking me what the issue was. I told him point-blank that the treatment was taking too long and suggested that we should try IUI (Intrauterine Insemination (IUI), which is a fertility treatment that involved placing sperm inside a woman's uterus to facilitate fertilization). I wanted to get the result fast not knowing that God had a better plan and that we were closer to our desired goal than when we started. Baba

My Journey to Motherhood

insisted that it was better he treated the underlying cause of infertility so that I could conceive naturally since he knew what the cause was and according to him, we had recorded a lot of improvement with the treatment and sooner than we expected, we would get a result. I left a bit hopeful after taking my injections with my both buttocks swollen from many injections. You can imagine taking an injection every week for 8 whole months. It wasn't easy. It was one of the prices we had to pay to get our desired result.

The same thing applies in life, nothing good comes easily. You have to pay the price to get whatever you desire, you have to be patient and persistent. Before you know it, your desire will be in your hands. What is that challenge you are going through? Be it infertility or other life challenges, don't give up. Keep pushing. You are closer to your result than when you started. Who knows, you might even be on the verge of getting that result and if you quit now, all your past efforts will be a waste and you might never achieve that result. So quitting is not an option. Instead, keep pushing.

Overcoming Infertility And Fibroid

9

Why Worry Over What You Don't Own?

—

I remember going to Baba's place one day feeling so dejected again. When he saw me, he asked me what the problem was. My 9th wedding anniversary was just a few weeks to this time, yet, there was no child to show for it. Baba, I am worried. He looked at me and said in his usual cool manner, "Why are you worrying yourself over what is not yours? Children are God's own. They are His heritage and He gives to what He wills. All you need do is to pray continuously that He remembers you and gives you children because if He decides otherwise, there is nothing you can do. So instead of worrying, just make yourself happy and pray to God to have mercy and make you fruitful."

Overcoming Infertility And Fibroid

He continued by giving me an analogy. He said, "You see, to prove that you are not the owners of these children, that we are just caretakers, I will give you this example."

"If a man buys the latest car and decides to destroy the car by smashing it with an axe, nobody will ask him. He can decide to destroy everything in one day by smashing the windscreen and other parts, people will only look and pass. After all, it's his car, he bought it with his money, he can do whatever he wants with it."

He continued, "But you can't give birth to a child today and decide to kill the child even if the child is just some hours old. If you do, you will be charged with murder and might eventually be killed if you try such. This is to prove that you don't own the child, you are just a caregiver for God. So stop worrying yourself. At the appointed time, He will give you children because he has said that none shall be barren. Just keep praying and doing the right thing as you are doing now and He will see your faith and heart and grant your heart's desires."

I thought about what he said and I saw a lot of sense in it. I decided to calm down and continue praying to God to have mercy and bless my womb. The Bible tells us in Psalms 127:3 that children are God's heritage and the fruit of the womb is a reward from God. God also tells us in the book of Ex. 23:26

that none shall be barren because the first commandment he gave to man after creation is "Be fruitful and multiply and replenish the earth." It's a commandment from Him, so we need not worry about ourselves. If this commandment is not coming to pass in our lives, then something is wrong somewhere. All we need to do is find out what is wrong by consulting our doctors and fertility specialists. Once these problems are fixed and the cause is addressed, then we will get the desired result by the grace of God.

Another thing I will advise is that, instead of getting worried over our inability to conceive, we should keep ourselves busy especially women. We can take courses, learn something new, start something, and be busy if we are not in any paid employment, just to keep ourselves busy. When you are busy, you have less time to think about the challenge of infertility. It was in the cause of this challenge that I started my business, Glomajos Enterprises where we produce various household cleaning products and also train those interested in our line of business. I made myself busy as much as I could. This does not mean that I didn't cry when I was alone sometimes. I did because I am human. I wet my pillow at night crying to God to give me children but I didn't take this inability as an excuse to stay idle. Let's get busy with our businesses and find time to see the doctor get a diagnosis. Thank God for doctors, God

My Journey to Motherhood

gave them to us because He knew that such challenges would occur. So, let's make the best use of them by getting the right diagnosis and following through with our treatment until we get the desired result. God will see us through and bless our wombs sooner that we expect by His grace.

I will conclude this chapter by admonishing us once more to stop worrying over what is not ours. Instead, we should take the right and necessary actions which will bring the desired result. The Bible has told us in the book of Matthew that no man can add a cubit to his years by worrying. Worrying is not good for any reason. Instead, it creates more problems than solutions. Instead of worrying, just hand everything over to God and be very patient while working with your doctor. Also, keep asking Him for the grace to scale through the waiting period because you sure need His grace to be in that waiting period with your sanity intact. I craved His grace so much during my waiting period and I specifically asked for the grace to be patient while working with my doctor. At last, I got pregnant at a time I was losing hope with the treatment. I pray God gives us all the grace we need to wait and in the end, we will testify by His grace.

Overcoming Infertility And Fibroid

10

God Answers Prayers...

―

Like I was narrating in chapter 8, we continued with the treatment by going to Dr. Ajayi's office at Mushin weekly for injections. We started going there in February 2019. We continued hoping that it would happen soon to the extent that our faith started waxing cold. My husband was getting discouraged but I would encourage him. Some days we didn't feel like going, we would encourage each other as we knew that it was a battle against infertility so we just had to keep fighting.

We would encourage each other like David in the Bible and continued that way until one morning in August 2019 when my landlord who coincidentally also happens to be my parish pastor in our local parish of The Redeemed Christian Church of God (RCCG) saw me said to me "Sister Ogechi, just be rejoicing and be thanking God because he has remembered you." I was looked at him and asked, "What do you mean sir?"

He said that they attended a program in another RCCG parish in Ikorodu, Lagos and that after the program, he went to see the man of God for something personal. Instead, the man of God told him that there was one of his neighbors that had been trusting God for the fruit of the womb and that he should tell me that God had answered my prayers. He said the pastor went ahead to describe me and even told him that I was fetching water from the tap within the compound at that moment, describing where the tap was situated at the entrance of the compound.

He advised me to go see that pastor. His wife came and we agreed on when to go because she had said that she would not be chanced the next Wednesday. I was surprised about how someone who I didn't know and haven't met before knew that I existed. I didn't even know that they held such a program nor that that parish existed. How can God reveal my case to a total stranger? Why not my pastors? If not that my pastor was one person I had a lot of respect for, I wouldn't have gone because, I was tired of my hope being raised each time and in the end, the waiting continued.

Overcoming Infertility And Fibroid

My Journey to Motherhood

When my husband came back, I told him what daddy (like we call our parish pastor) had told me and he encouraged me to go and see the pastor because God can decide to use anybody. He is unquestionable. I agreed and went with my pastor's wife on the day we agreed to go. That Wednesday, the 28th of August 2019 was exactly two weeks to my 9th wedding anniversary which is September 11th. I cried and asked God when this would end. I never knew that the end was very close. I cried so much in the church that day. I remembered all that I had been through in the past years. Our effort, the money we spent, and everything that yielded no result, and in just two weeks, it would be my 9th wedding anniversary.

At this point, I began to remember my friends that got married after me. Most of them had at least 3 children. Jane, who was my chief bride's maid had four children at that time even though she got married about a year I did. As all these memories came to mind, I was cried and it was intensified by my love for children. I was the head of the children department in my area that comprises 3 RCCG parishes where I was taking care of children while I didn't have my biological children. After the program, we waited to see the pastor and he prayed for me telling me not to worry but to continue thanking God because He had answered my prayers. Thereafter, we left.

Overcoming Infertility And Fibroid

My Journey to Motherhood

Another thing happened in September 2019, 24th September to be precise. Someone had seen my page on Instagram (www.instagram.com/glomajos) because I took a workshop on how to produce soap and other household cleaning products holding both online and offline classes. She reached out to me telling me that she would like to learn how to make soap. We negotiated the fee and agreed on the time because it was going to be an online class since she was not residing in Lagos. We were about ending the chat when I asked for her name so that I could add her to my contact. She said her name was Apostle so and so. I thanked her for visiting our page and reaching out. The next question she asked was, can I pray for you? I said why not so she said let's pray. The next statement from her was "I can see a baby, do you want a baby?" I was shocked to my bone marrow and I became afraid. Could this be a scammer? How did she know that I needed a baby? Did she want to use soap training as an entry just to exploit me? So many questions were growing through my mind. I responded by saying yes, and she prayed for me that God would grant my prayers. I gave her my account number to pay for the training and we ended the chat.

Overcoming Infertility And Fibroid

My Journey to Motherhood

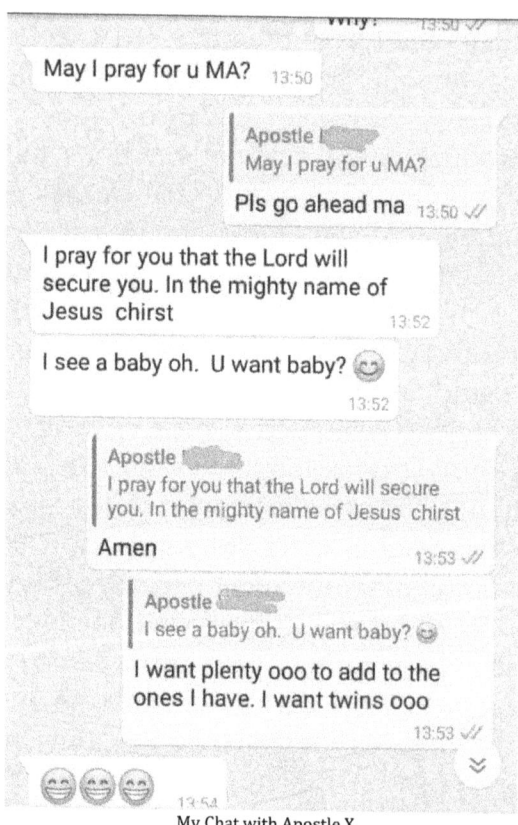

My Chat with Apostle X

Immediately, I turned to my husband who was sitting by and told him what has just happened, he was also surprised and said I shouldn't be carried away, that it could be someone that knew me disguised as a stranger. While we were still talking, the alert of her payment came in and we became more

Overcoming Infertility And Fibroid

confused. We didn't know what to believe. My husband advised that I should tread with caution while dealing with her but to my amazement, she never brought the subject up again all through the period of the training. God revealing my case to another stranger this time, someone outside Lagos, someone in the North that got to me only through social media for another purpose was a confirmation of what the pastor in Ikorodu said.

Who said God does not answer prayers? No wonder He says we should not be weary of doing good and that in due course, we will be rewarded. So I am also admonishing you right now to keep at the good thing you are doing, God sees and he answers prayers. Keep at it, see your doctor, continue your medication, keep yourself busy, and make yourself happy. In no time, you will get answers to your prayers.

Overcoming Infertility And Fibroid

My Journey to Motherhood

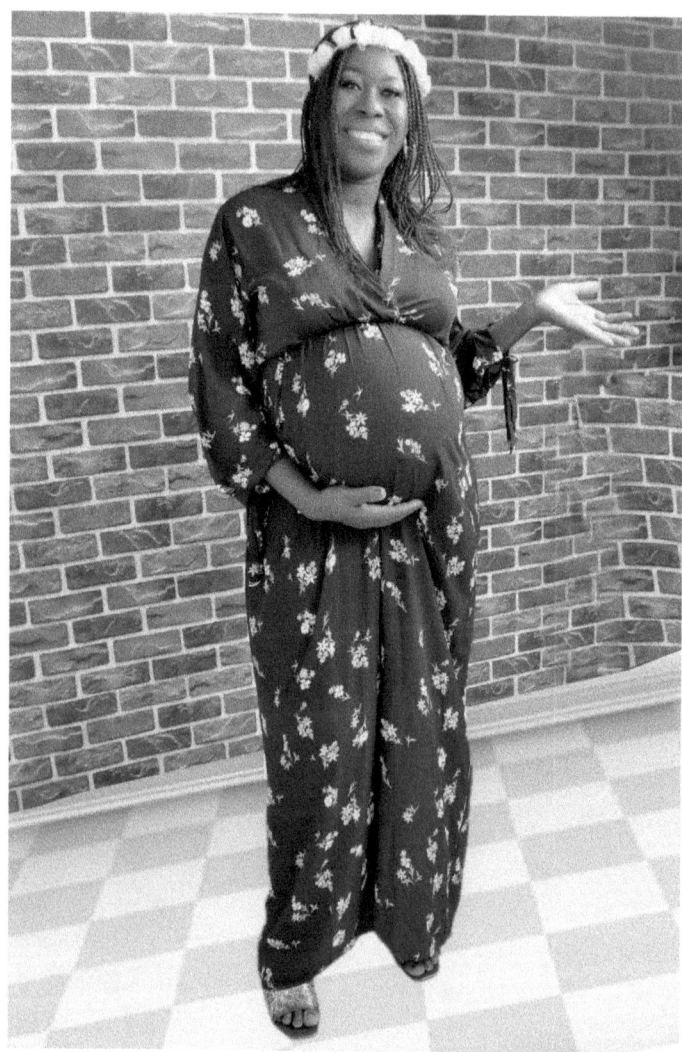

During Pregnancy

Overcoming Infertility And Fibroid

11

And It Happened...

—

So after all this, life continued. I went about my routine but I kept praying that God honors His word. For Him to speak through different strangers, I was sure that my answer was very close. What did I do? I changed my attitude from that of request to praise and thanksgiving. I kept thanking him for what He decided to do even though I had not seen it yet. The first Sunday in September 2019, which was a Thanksgiving Sunday, I had gone out to testify and to thank God for keeping my husband and me for these nine years despite the challenges. Someone once asked me what I was even celebrating the previous year when I was happy on our 8th wedding anniversary. I responded by telling the person that I was celebrating God's faithfulness to my family and for keeping us together despite the challenges. We had every reason to be grateful. I reminded the person of the Bible passage that says "A living dog is better than a dead lion." So, as far as God has kept both of us alive, that means He would perfect all other things.

Screenshot of my 9th year anniversary on Facebook

In this particular thanksgiving service in September 2019, I rolled on the floor at the altar before the congregation appreciating God for all he had done for the previous 9 years and for what he was yet to do. I decided to put praise to my challenges because I believe where prayer is taking too long, I

My Journey to Motherhood

should try praise. I was rolling on the floor thanking him and professing that tomorrow would be greater than today. I had given the song to the person in the engine room to play it for me when it was my turn to testify. On the D-day, September 11th, 2019, I had gone on Facebook to announce that it was my wedding anniversary but I wanted people to appreciate God on our behalf rather than pray for us. I was full of joy thanks to God that day.

Then suddenly in October 2019, towards the time of my monthly menstrual cycle, I started to have feeling. I was becoming weak and experiencing some changes in my body. However, I was not bothered because we had experienced such so many times in the past. I was at home on the 17th of October feeling the heaviness in my breast and other symptoms. I decided to carry out a home test and it came out negative. The next day was Friday. I couldn't stand from my bed and I couldn't go out either. I was just thinking and crying, remembering that exactly 9 months then, I would be forty years old and yet, I had no biological child to show for it. I was home alone that day. I cried so much that I couldn't go to my office that day. I got married at thirty in 2010 and here it was looking like I would not have my child by the time I would be forty because this was October already.

Two days later, 20th October 2019 is a date I would never forget all my life. I woke around 5:30am to start preparing for church service that day. I needed to be in church by 7am to join the workers' meeting. I had a dream that night but I forgot it immediately I woke. As I was heading to the bathroom, I had a very strong urge to repeat the pregnancy test. By this time, my period that was supposed to start three days earlier had not started but it was nothing to me because my period had once been delayed for nine days in the past. When we thought that it had finally happened, after nine days of delay, the period started. So this one was just three days and I was therefore not bothered. When I got that urge to repeat the test, I refused and told myself that I didn't want to cry again or be distracted. However, I surrendered to the urge and decided to do the test. After all, I just bought a new pack of pregnancy test kit that had 50 test sticks.

I took one and went into the bathroom for testing. Suddenly, my eyes went to where I dropped the test stick and I saw two bold red lines signaling a positive result. I couldn't believe what I was seeing. I stood up, bathed, picked it up, and ran to the bedroom where my husband was still sleeping. I woke him up in excitement telling him that I had just tested positive for a pregnancy test. He looked at me and told me that he would not believe me until I confirmed it with a blood test. I didn't mind him as I knew what I saw. Before this time, I had NEVER in my nine years of marriage tested positive at any time so I knew what I saw. I just went on the floor in the room,

My Journey to Motherhood

rolling and thanking my God. I was so happy. This was a day I looked forward to, for the past nine years. I was happy that it finally came to pass.

I dressed up and went to church that day full of excitement and beaming smiles. I couldn't blame my husband for his disbelief. When I got to the church, I went to my auntie, my uncle's wife, and told her what happened. I told her that I just tested positive for a pregnancy test that morning and she told me that she dreamt and saw me carrying twins during the week. I was so happy. I couldn't discuss it with any other person yet, so I just kept it to myself and even told my auntie not to tell my uncle yet.

Two days after was a Tuesday. I went to Dr. Ajayi and told him what happened. He carried out a pregnancy test using blood as a sample this time and it came out POSITIVE. I was filled with joy. I ran home and waited for my husband to come back and I showed him the result. He couldn't hide his joy. It was that moment we had anticipated for nine years and finally, it happened. My husband is an Igbo man and the first son for that matter. Yet, God gave us the patience to wait on Him these nine years not minding what people were saying, even when they came with different advice telling us of places to go that were not godly. We refused because we knew that it was only God that gives children.

Overcoming Infertility And Fibroid

My Journey to Motherhood

So I am praying for you that are going through this same challenge right now or any challenge at all. God will show up for you when you least expect. I see you becoming a biological parent in Jesus' mighty name. God that did it for us will do it for you also in Jesus' mighty name.

Overcoming Infertility And Fibroid

12

And The Devil Came With Blighted Ovum...

With the excitement caused by the confirmation that I was pregnant, we decided it was best to register for antenatal early enough because of my age and the number of years it took us to achieve this. So at 6 weeks 5 days pregnant, I went to the hospital to register for antenatal. We had decided we would use a government hospital as we believed they would have the needed expertise to handle my case. We preferred those tertiary hospitals which was why I used Lagos University Teaching Hospital (LUTH) when I had the myomectomy.

One of the prerequisites for registering for antenatal was a scan to confirm the condition and timing of the pregnancy, so

My Journey to Motherhood

I was sent to go for a scan. During the scan, the sonographer told me that she could only see an empty sac as she could neither see the fetal pole nor the baby's heartbeat. She wrote in her report that it was a blighted ovum. She asked me to repeat the scan in two weeks. I had not come across that word before so I searched for it on Google to read about it. I contacted my doctor friend in LUTH and told him about it. He said at 6 weeks, the fetal pole ought to be seen. He then advised me to rather wait for one week to repeat the scan and if the same thing occurred, I should evacuate it to give room for another pregnancy.

All I was read was negative and unpleasant. Not satisfied, I went to my group that supported those trying to conceive on Facebook to ask what it was, if anyone had experienced it before and how it ended. Most of the responses I got were negative.

I called doctor Ajayi on our way back to tell him what the scan result was and he asked me to come the next morning. I got home, went on my knees, and prayed to God in tears, asking Him to have mercy on me and make my case end in. I cried until I was tired. However, my husband would look at me and say "Except it's not from God. If it's from God then it's perfected, nothing will happen to it." He was so sure and unshaken in his faith. The next morning, he got to Dr. Ajayi's place and told him what happened. Meanwhile, I was still at

Overcoming Infertility And Fibroid

home and was too weak to stand because of my crying and confusion. My husband called me to join him at Baba's place. I managed to take my bath, got ready, and went there. Baba gave me an injection assuring me that it would be fine by the grace of God.

I left for home. Those two weeks were the longest two weeks so far. I cried and prayed. I was so confused. We soaked ourselves in prayers. We told a few of our pastors including the pastor that first gave the revelation and we were all praying and asking God for mercy. Remember we had also done our part by going to Dr. Ajayi, so you do your part while you pray to God and He would do His. Those two weeks were the longest for me as I was so afraid and confused. When I went back, lo and behold, my baby was intact! I couldn't hide my joy. I shouted, praising God at the top of my voice that sonographer was wondering why I was shouting. I told her that it took us 9 whole years to achieve that pregnancy and she started praising God with me.

What Is a Blighted Ovum?

According to webMD.com, a blighted ovum occurs when a fertilized egg is implanted in the uterus but doesn't develop into an embryo. It is also referred to as an anembryonic (no embryo) pregnancy and is a leading cause of early pregnancy failure or miscarriage. Often, it occurs so early that you don't even know you are pregnant.

According to healthline.com, a blighted ovum is a fertilized egg that implants itself in the uterus but doesn't become an embryo. The placenta and embryonic sac form but remain empty. There's no growing baby. It's also known as anembryonic gestation or anembryonic pregnancy. You can go to Google to read more about this condition because knowledge is very powerful.

After all of these, God gave us victory and my case ended in praise. As I type this, that baby that the devil tried to toil with is a very pretty princess and she is one month old already. My advice to you is, do your part, see the right doctor and pray. God will do His part as there is nothing impossible for Him to do. He will turn your mourning to dancing and give you beauty for ashes as you remain patient with him in Jesus' mighty, name.

Overcoming Infertility And Fibroid

13

And It's a girl...

By the grace of God Almighty, I finally put a beautiful bouncing baby girl to bed a few days after my 40th Birthday in June 2020, proof that God does not look at age when he is set to carry out His work.

Doctors have always told us that as a woman approaches her late 30's, her chances of getting pregnant reduces. According to the Centers for Disease Control and Prevention, 30% of women ages 40 to 44 will experience infertility. Your chances of conceiving in any given month are also lower once you go beyond the big 40.

My Journey to Motherhood

A 40-year-old only has a 5% chance of getting pregnant per month. This means that even for those that would get pregnant, it may take longer.

God did mine when I was over 39 years old. I conceived for the first time in our 9 years of marriage. I had a very stress free pregnancy. I neither vomited nor spat for one day. There was no morning sickness and I was strong all through. This is to tell you that there is nothing that God cannot do. Depend totally on Him and he would see you through. God gave me my daughter as my 40th Birthday gift. He will surprise you too. As I mentioned earlier, only ensure that you are doing something to take you closer to the result you desire. Don't just sit and do nothing. Ensure you and your partner are seeing the right doctor and doing what you are asked to do.

Overcoming Infertility And Fibroid

My Journey to Motherhood

Celebrating my 40th Birthday

I know it's not easy and even the money spent on the journey is another major challenge. The cost of running several tests is not cheap. Even the medical personnel do not help the

Overcoming Infertility And Fibroid

My Journey to Motherhood

matter as they ask you to go for a test and won't interpret or explain the result to you. People around may not be supportive. They may have called you names and mocked you, but don't be discouraged. It's only God that gives children, you'll give your testimony soon.

I join my faith with yours and I pray that every obstacle stopping you from becoming a mother is uprooted in Jesus' mighty name. You will carry and nurse your baby in Jesus' mighty name. Your age doesn't matter. We recently heard of a 67-year-old mother who gave birth to twins. If He can do hers, He will do yours also.

When I couldn't go for antenatal anymore because of the Covid-19 pandemic, I registered for an online antenatal with Ask the Gynecologists, a group on Facebook that educates people about fertility. There is a lady in the group who got married for the first time at 46 years old and she gave birth at 47. It's only God that can do this.

Overcoming Infertility And Fibroid

My Journey to Motherhood

When I asked about Blighted Ovum on facebook

I have encouraged you with my story by telling you what we did wrong and how we corrected it. Just ensure that you are not sitting and doing nothing. Do something. Keep yourself busy, see your doctor, take action and my Father in Heaven will supply ALL your needs; physical, spiritual, marital, financial, and all in Jesus' name. Remember the story of

Overcoming Infertility And Fibroid

Lazarus in the Bible. Before Jesus got there he was dead already. Jesus wept and asked them to take away the stone. He then prayed and Lazarus came back to life. There are certain miracles that God may not do until we play our part and take away the stone before he performs His miracle. You may have a role to play for your miracle to be achieved.

I will be stopping here till we meet again either by you writing to me or calling to share your testimony because God will bless every expectant womb reading this book, including YOU. You are the next in line to testify.

Baby dust to all trying to conceive as parents.

Overcoming Infertility And Fibroid

Milton Keynes UK
Ingram Content Group UK Ltd.
UKHW021126030424
440506UK00009B/1213

9 798687 516778